CONRAD DEAS

FOREWORD BY HAL ELROD, AUTHOR OF *THE MIRACLE MORNING*

HUSBAND

ON

PURPSE

YOUR 30 DAY ACTION PLAN TO BECOME A BETTER MAN AND BUILD A BETTER MARRIAGE

ISBN-13: 978-0692522615

ISBN-10: 0692522611

First Edition: September 2015

10 9 8 7 6 5 4 3 2 1

Visit

www.HusbandOnPurpose.com/free-book-bonuses

to claim
A Free Audio Summary of The Book

**The Digital 12 Month Husband On Purpose
Journal and Worksheets**

**Weekly Stories from other husbands being
purposeful about their marriages**

**And a $100 Gift (real world value) reserved
only for The Husband On Purpose
Community Participants**

Join the community. Get the goods.
Become a Better Man. Build a Better Marriage

www.HusbandOnPurpose.com/free-book-bonuses

Dedicated to
Jennifer, Jalen, A.C., and Andrew

I love you all more than words can express. My hope is that I can be
exactly who you need me to be, to help you become exactly who you
were created to be. This book is a part of that process.

CONTENTS

Your 30 Day Challenge

The Ben Franklin Method To Being a Husband On Purpose

The Husband On Purpose 30 Day Challenge

Sample Journal

Foreword

You know as well as I do: happy wife = happy life. Yet, as husbands and human beings, we often choose being right or being selfish or being lazy over being a great husband and doing that which will make our marriage flourish.

In Husband On Purpose, Conrad Deas has given us the step-by-step blueprint that can quickly transform your marriage by transforming who you're being.

Remember that who we're being—or becoming—is always more important than what we're doing, and yet it is what we're doing that's determining who we're becoming.

This book tells you exactly what you need to do in order to become the husband you're capable of being, who can create the marriage you've always wanted. As soon as you do, and you can literally start the day you begin reading this book, you will become the man of your wife's dreams—the guy she fell in love with and married so long ago.

As the sole provider for my wife and our two children, I always thought my #1 role in life was just that—provider. Then, a conversation with my good friend and fellow family man, Jon Vroman, enlightened me to a new perspective: My #1 role and priority in life is to be the best husband/father that I can possibly be, and being a "provider" is only a sub-role of being a great husband/father.

I realized that supporting my wife and positively influencing my children through the quality time I spend with them— FULLY PRESENT & ENGAGED—is the most value I can give to my family.

Think about it. Ten years from now, your wife (and kids, if you have any) aren't going to remember how many mortgage payments you made. They're going to remember the impact you made in their lives, based on how engaged you were with them. They're going to remember how you made them feel, how supportive you were, and the role you played in their personal development.

Another realization I had, that was so effectively articulated and reinforced in Conrad's book, is that creating and maintaining a successful marriage is 100% our responsibility and that we can literally create or "generate" anything we want for our marriage in any moment.

My marriage mantra reminds me of this each morning when I read it: *"I am committed to being the perfect husband today, so that my wife and I experience the extraordinary marriage that we both want and deserve. If it is to be, it is up to me, and my wife will respond accordingly."*

Husband On Purpose will help you become a better you so you can be a better husband and build a better marriage.

- Hal Elrod, author of *The Miracle Morning*

Preface

This book started as a string of emails between myself and a few friends. I was either currently going through, or recently completed, my first 30 Day challenge of being a Husband On Purpose.

I was experiencing changes in my marriage that I wasn't even aware needed to take place. These changes had such an impact on me that I had to share with my friends what was happening.

I've kept the content of what you're about to read exactly like, or very similar to, my original conversations with my friends. I expanded on a few things to hopefully explain them better, while trying to keep the same conversational feel. So this is really just a conversation between you and me.

My hope is that you will walk away from this conversation encouraged, uplifted, and educated on how you might become a better you and as a result become a better husband, who loves your wife on purpose, and builds a better marriage that benefits you both.

Now... let's talk.

From Laying in Your Own Poop to Being an Accomplished Man

Approximately 20 - 50 years ago, a kid was born. To protect the innocent, let's call him Jack. Jack couldn't do anything but poop, pee, sleep, eat, and cry, like every other kid.

A few months later, Jack thought it may be possible for him to move on his own like the big people around him. So he tried to move. And he failed. He tried to move again. And he failed again. Jack figured out moving one way wasn't going to work, so he tried to move a different way. After many attempts, many failures, and many reattempts, one day…

Jack rolled over!!!

He's on the move now. Well not really, but he thinks he is. Jack figures, *"If I can roll over maybe I can actually get to everything these big people never take me to!"*

So he tries to move a different way. And you guessed it, he fails. All he can do is roll over. Jack gets frustrated, he cries, and he keeps trying to move. Weeks go by and finally…

Jack scoots!!! It's not much, but he's one centimeter closer to everything he's not supposed to touch! Jack is making progress.

Eventually, Jack learns how to scoot faster and further. And eventually he learns how to crawl and soon he's touching everything he's not supposed to.

And finally after stumbling, falling, and enduring the humiliation of not getting it right the first few times, Jack figures out how to walk. The same kid who couldn't even face a different way just a few months ago, is now getting his hands into everything he dreamed about before.

You were Jack. You went from eat, sleep, poop, and pee all day to walking around getting in trouble in a relatively short amount of time.

How did you go from laying in your own poop to the accomplished man you are today?

How did you go from not being able to move, to turning over? From not being able to scoot, to walking? From being scared to talk to girls, to marrying your wife?

As you've progressed through life, everything that you couldn't do before and can do now, are things you've accomplished.

You've accomplished a lot, so congratulations!

One of your biggest accomplishments, and I hope you'd agree, is marrying your wife. At some point you two probably didn't know each other. Eventually you got to know each other and somehow you convinced her to spend the rest of her life alongside you.

From learning to walk and not poop on yourself, to marrying your wife... What do all these things have in common?

You did them On Purpose.

Whether you wanted to gain something, or avoid something, you purposefully did whatever you had to do, to accomplish what you set out to do.

In the dating stages we do a lot of stuff on purpose. We make sure our potential wife knows that we want to be with her. We show her that she is important to us. We make sure she knows we love her. She doesn't have to question whether or not we want to be with her.

We do all of this... On Purpose.

We date her On Purpose and eventually we get married On Purpose.

Unfortunately, as my friend Donnie Bryant said, *"Most of us get married on purpose... then we end up being a husband on accident."*

Why is that? How do we go from being so purposeful to being so thoughtless?

Well it's pretty easy actually. From my own experience and what other husbands have told me, it's easy to slip back into a mode of the mundane, operate on autopilot, and get stuck in a rut. With the pressure of all the perceived responsibilities of being a husband, is it a wonder that you can forget to actually be a husband?

In the following pages and the included resources you will learn what other husbands are doing to get out of autopilot mode and make sure our wives know we don't take them for granted. You will learn the great loving habits that we're establishing to last a lifetime. You will get ideas on how we avoid the ruts that used to keep us doing the same things in the same ways.

After reading this you'll know how to discover the specific steps that can help you become a "hero" in your wife's eyes.

You'll learn what we did and what we're doing to be Husbands On Purpose. This book is not about theory and as you'll see I've come to learn that guessing is a waste of time. You're about to get actionable steps that you can test for yourself.

If the specifics steps I took and take don't work for you, you'll know how to discover the steps that will work for you.

You are invited to join a community of men that will help keep you on the track of being a better husband no matter what your specific steps are. You will learn how to guarantee your wife knows that she is more important than anything else in your life. She will know that she has your attention and you'll learn how to communicate with her better. You will learn how to overcome problems and challenges quicker than you ever have. You will finally have a better understanding of your wife and her needs. You'll also be able and willing to communicate your needs to her.

You will learn how to work on yourself, to benefit your wife.

If you've ever heard your wife say, *"I just don't feel connected to you"* or anything similar, Husband On Purpose shows you how to turn that feeling around for the both of you. This is the process I used to go from my wife telling me that she felt "distant and not connected" to me, to a month later her telling me *"You have been great, I trust you more, I'm grateful for the turnaround in our marriage and relationship. I'm so happy with where we're headed..."*

The month of my 30th birthday I had this "genius" thought come to me that I wanted to make sure my wife knew she was loved by me and never had to second guess that.

Six months after my 30th birthday, I was at one of the lowest points in my marriage. I failed.

Seven months after my 30th birthday, I had a better marriage than I even knew was possible!

With the dramatic shift that happened in my marriage I had to share it with a few others. Now I'm sharing it with you. I look forward to you having your own success story very soon.

My mission is to help you become a better you so you can be a better husband and build a better marriage. If you're a better husband who builds a better marriage you can help make your

14

wife better. If you help make your wife better, you can both help make your home better. If your home is better, your home can help make your community better. If your community is better your community can help make the world better because the world is made up of communities, which are made up of homes, which are made up of you.

It all starts with you.

How Dare I Try to Help Others!?

There are several challenges when it comes to writing a book like this. I faced three that seemed major while I was overcoming them and minor once I moved beyond them.

The first thing I worried about was being "qualified". Then I remembered, I already did what you're about to do.

Have I done it perfectly? Absolutely not. I've done it through imperfections.

Additionally, bits and pieces of this information has already helped others. Now it's all together in one resource for you since there is a chance that you and I may not have a one on one conversation.

Then I wondered if the information was "enough". The truth is, if I wrote you a 100 word essay that helped you with actionable steps to improve your marriage, it would be "enough".

It's not the amount of information, but what you do with the information that makes a difference. The words on this page, or any page, are just information.

Knowledge is what you gain after doing what you learn from the information.

Knowledge really is power. The reason people think it's not is because they mistake information for knowledge.

If you read just 10 words and you apply the information you

receive from those 10 words, gain some knowledge, and that knowledge helps change your life for the rest to your life, it is "enough" information.

My BIGGEST challenge was having "setbacks" in my own marriage while writing this book. The first time I went through the 30 day challenge you'll learn about, my wife and I had a few arguments during that 30 days. Fortunately, at that time we overcame those arguments and disagreements quicker than any other time in our marriage that I could remember before that.

During that first 30 Days, this book did not exist though. Not in the cloud. Not on a hard drive. Not even in my mind. I was doing the challenge because I wanted to just love my wife on purpose in a more structured way.

However, by the time I was doing subsequent 30 day challenges in trying to solidify my habits and other people knew about the challenge, and some were doing their own challenges, this book was being written. It was then that the setbacks started to bother me. By this time my wife knew about the book as well.

It quickly became discouraging trying to help others in an area where I felt I was constantly having setbacks.

My marriage was definitely better than before. We had better communication, better intimacy, a tighter bond, and just a more fulfilling relationship overall. Yet for some reason the setbacks, arguments and disagreements, were magnified in my mind.

Fortunately we got over them extremely quick most of the time. Despite resolving them quickly, it would still cause mental blocks for me in putting together a book about helping men have a better marriage.

I don't think anyone is supposed to have a perfect marriage, yet the setbacks still contributed to my lack of feeling "qualified" and if the information I was sharing was "enough".

I had to remember that *"The problem is NEVER the problem. The problem is ALWAYS how you think about the problem."* – **Dan Sullivan**

Being a Husband On Purpose is not about eliminating all of your problems before they come up, but about working with your wife and growing through problems when they do come up.

I share that to say, first of all you're dealing with a regular guy like you. I'm not perfect and my marriage is as imperfect as I am. I've used the information on these pages to help better my marriage and continue to do so today and will continue to do so as long as my wife and I live.

I have setbacks and will assume you will too. If you find a way not to, please let me know. I have a few friends and thousands of people in similar situations that would like to know how you make that happen.

Once, a mentor told me that a rocket ship is off course ninety plus percent of the time and only makes it to its destination by constantly making small adjustments as it constantly moves forward.

Fortunately, you and I don't have to be off course ninety plus percent of time, but we do have to make constant adjustments as we move forward to make it to our destination. The information in this book is here to help you make some of those slight, and sometimes dramatic, adjustments.

In the next few pages you'll learn the question I had to ask myself that helped change everything in my marriage. You'll learn a 60 second technique to keep good situations from getting bad and bad situations from getting worse. You'll learn how you can appear to read your wife's mind and make her fall in love with you like it's the first time. You'll learn exactly what I did to go from seeing my wife with one of the most

17

disappointed looks on her face telling me she felt disconnected from me, to less than 30 days later getting random messages from her expressing how much she loves me and how she feels more connected to me than ever.

One thing I must say before we continue. If your marriage is on the verge of divorce, please go seek personal professional counseling. I'd encourage you to still read this book and implement what you learn and to seek assistance from a trained professional. I am in no way a trained therapist, psychologist, and the only government issued license I have right now is to operate a motor vehicle. I'm just sharing what helped and is helping my marriage and other marriages around the globe.

Questions to Increase the Quality of Your Marriage

"Quality questions create a quality life. Successful people ask better questions, and as a result, they get better answers." - Tony Robbins

1

Tip The First Domino

Extraordinary results require you to go small.

- The ONE Thing

In every area of your life there is something that makes the biggest difference or has the most impact right now. In July of 2013 Michael J. Maher introduced me to a book called *The ONE Thing* by Gary Keller and Jay Papasan. The book is based on what they call the "focusing question" or as I like to call it, The First Domino.

How can you knock over a domino the size of the Leaning Tower of Pisa? Gary and Jay illustrate in their book that a domino is capable of knocking over another domino that is 50% larger than itself. If you start with a two-inch domino and keep increasing them by 50%, the 18th domino would be the size of the Leaning Tower of Pisa and the 17th domino would knock it down. So how do you knock over a 180 foot tall domino? You tip the two-inch domino first.

In *The ONE Thing*, the first domino looks like this, "What's the ONE thing that I can do, such that by doing it, everything else becomes easier or unnecessary?" That one question is used to help you identify and focus on the ONE thing that has the biggest impact in different areas of your life right now.

There's HUGE power in asking this question, especially in your marriage.

In relation to your marriage, the first domino looks like this, "What's the ONE Thing I can do in my marriage, such that by doing it, everything else becomes easier or unnecessary?"

When I first heard this question my marriage was actually in a pretty good place. Well at least I thought it was.

Months later I finally read *The ONE Thing* and I started to ask myself the question so I could begin tipping the first domino in my marriage.

After a lot of prayer, reflection, and remembering something one of my best friends told me once, the answer I felt God gave me was "Love her". But not only Love her, make sure that she knows without a hint of doubt that you love her.

Before I got married, a very good friend told me, "You know I always try to make sure my wife never has to ask the question, 'Does he love me?'" He told me that long before I was married and it stuck with me for years. Thanks Artice!

I started to remember all the books I read before marriage and since being married, and how Love is what my wife probably needs most in our relationship.

So I felt God was telling me, by making absolutely sure your wife absolutely knows you love her and never has to wonder do you love her, everything else will be easier or unnecessary.

You can take this question as far as you want to go.

The next step in the question would be, "What's the ONE thing I can do to Love My Wife, such that by doing it, everything else would be easier or unnecessary?"

Read *The ONE Thing* for a deep dive into this question and

how it can help you in other areas of your life.

Finish this book first.

I tried, or at least I thought I tried, to make sure she knew I loved her starting back around the end of February or beginning of March. Things would seem to be going good then a "hiccup" would happen and I would let it be a reason for me to stop trying to make sure she knew.

Then I would hop back on the train of making sure she felt loved. Then I would fall off again.

Hop on. Hop off. It was a bad habit, but I honestly thought I was doing a pretty good job.

Until that HORRIBLE day in the bathroom in August.

One day we were standing in our bathroom. I believe we were getting ready to go somewhere. I was probably trimming my beard and she was probably putting on makeup.

I can't remember exactly what we were doing because I got hit with a 2x4 smack dab across the forehead!

It wasn't a real 2x4, but that could have been better.

We're getting ready, in what I thought was a happy moment. My wife looks at me and she says to me *"I don't feel connected to you. I feel distant from you."*

BAM!

After months of making sure she knew she was loved (or so I thought) she hits me with *"I don't feel connected or close."*

How does that happen!?

But that wasn't the 2x4 that smacked me in the face.

Remember I thought I was doing a pretty good job. I thought we were in a pretty good place. So I asked her, "Why do you feel that way?"

She couldn't explain to me why she felt that way at that specific moment. So I foolishly conclude that it's not my fault she feels that way.

I honestly felt it wasn't. So I honestly decided to smack myself in the face with a 2x4.

I say, *"That sounds like a personal problem you need to deal with on your own."*

Wow...

Yes I did...

Yes I was an idiot.

I'm not sure what I was thinking LOL, but that's what I said.

I can laugh about it now, but it was absolutely no laughing matter when it happened.

After removing the splinters from my face, God convicted me and I realized it didn't matter if it was my fault or not (even though it probably was).

It was my responsibility.

What kind of chump husband doesn't take responsibility for the way his wife feels about their marriage?

Not me! Anymore.

So at the end of August I challenged myself to purposefully be a better husband and make sure she knew with no doubt in her mind that she was absolutely loved every single day for 30 days straight.

I already knew that doing this would make everything else in our marriage easier or unnecessary. What I didn't know was that by making sure it was done consistently every single day would take me from a HORRIBLE bathroom experience and what I felt was one of the lowest points in my marriage, to 30 days later us both feeling more fulfilled than we ever had before and with an even brighter future to look towards.

So how did I go from sucking as a husband to sucking less?

I asked another question.

2

Speak Her Dialect

What changed after 6 months of trying and not doing?

Well first, it was I felt convicted that I knew this was something God told me would make a difference in my marriage and I still hadn't done it fully.

On top of that my wife felt distant from me and couldn't tell me why.

For six months I tried to make sure she knew I loved her, but I would get discouraged and stop. I knew I needed to be consistent, so I told myself I need to do it for 30 days straight.

But do what?

I knew I needed to make sure she knew she was loved without a hint of doubt, but how?

Well I knew her Love Languages and I was pretty sure I understood her dialects of each language.

If you're not familiar with the term "Love Languages" you should absolutely pick up Dr. Gary Chapman's *The Five Love Languages* after you finish this one.

I was fortunate enough that a mentor of mine had me read

)ook, for business purposes, long before I got married.

A few lines from now you'll see why you don't need to read the book right now. I'm going to tell you how to cheat.

If you're familiar with the book, but don't remember the part about dialects here's a brief reminder.

Everyone in America doesn't speak the same English. I'm from Charleston, SC and when I went to spend the summer 90 minutes up the highway in Columbia, SC, I was always reminded that I spoke a different dialect. Now imagine when I went to New York or if I had went to California. We all speak English, but we speak different dialects based on who we are and where we're from.

Dialects work the same way in your marriage. If your wife's Love Language is Quality Time, her "dialect" of quality time is not the same as everyone else's dialect of quality time and may not be the same as what you're thinking.

I thought I knew my wife's dialects and how to speak them, but instead of guessing what to do to speak her Love Language specifically, I cheated.

I decided to just ask her.

Why guess when you can know?

I sent her an email asking her to finish this statement "I ABSOLUTELY know my husband loves me when..."

Fortunately for me, my wife rarely has trouble expressing herself. She sent me back a paragraph that I was able to take out eight different things I could do to show her I love her and make sure she knew it.

I asked her in an email so I could have access to it later. I wanted it in writing so I didn't have to try and remember everything she was going to say.

This same sentence has not worked as well for a few of my friends, but the premise is to get your wife to tell you in detail what makes her feel loved and when she ABSOLUTELY knows she is loved, whether it's something you currently do or something she would like you to do.

My wife's eight things were a mixture of things I already did and things I know I didn't do enough. One of my friends said he got back a one sentence answer, so he obviously needed to probe a little more. I had to probe on certain things, like one thing my wife mentioned was "when my husband is thoughtful", so I just had to ask her, "What does being thoughtful look like to you?"

You may feel silly or foolish having to ask her specifically how to love her.

That's pride. Be humble.

She may want you to just "read her mind". That would be nice. And a little later I'll show you how to appear like you can, but for now just ask.

I took the eight things from her email response and put them in a list numbered 1-8 that I stuck in a "Notes" app on my phone so I could easily access the list.

Just about every day I looked over this list, prayed about the things on it, thought about them, asked myself questions about them, and chose one of them per day to do for my wife.

Now it's your turn. Email your wife asking her to finish one of these statements…

I ABSOLUTELY know my husband loves me when…
or
I ABSOLUTELY feel loved by my husband when...

If she doesn't respond within 24 hours, send a follow up text message, saying something like, "Hey no rush, but I wanted to make sure you got that email about when you feel loved. I want to really make sure I do "Us" ON PURPOSE so when you can, please email me that back so I can have it for future reference. Love you :-). You did get the email right?"

You want to ask the challenge question via email so she can answer at her convenience and you can have a copy you can easily access later.

Email also implies that the answer can be as long as she wants it to be. If you send the question via text message she may feel the answer needs to be shorter since she's answering via text.

Don't ask her the question verbally. At least not initially. Have a conversation about it later if you want to, but get her answer in written format first.

You need to make a list of the answers your wife gives you. A physical list either in your journal, a notebook, your phone, or use the *Exactly How to Speak* section in this book.

Don't try to store her answers in your mind. We're talking about being a Husband On Purpose.

You need to purposefully write down her list so you can purposefully free your mind to come up with creative ways to implement what is on her list.

Your mind is better used for thinking about how you can implement the things on her list rather than trying to remember the things on her list.

The list is not for you to check things off. Your list gives you the boundaries in which to create your specific actions you're going to take.

You can create and do things that add no value to your wife, or you can create and do things that are in alignment with what your wife wants.

There were other things I did for myself each day, but the purpose of doing anything else was trying to do one of her eight things each day. It took a lot of prayer, some creativity, and some help from Google, but I did something every day for 30 days to show her I loved her and make sure that she knew it.

What was the difference between this time and the previous months where I failed to be consistent?

One big difference was I specifically spoke her Love Languages and didn't have to guess at how to speak them.

Additionally, I did a few simple things to better myself every day that helped me stay on track with speaking her Love Languages specifically. You'll discover those changes in just a few pages from now.

Those steps helped me DISARM things that were BS from my marriage. You're about to learn how to do the same.

You may be saying, like other husbands have said to me, "I already know when my wife feels loved. I already know what to do"

Great!

Ask her how to speak her dialect anyway.

Obviously there is value in the question itself and the answer she gives you.

However, there is also value in the actual asking of the question.

There is value in the way your wife will feel being able to express herself. There is value in her knowing that you actually want to know what makes her feel loved. There is value in her hearing (or reading) you ask her how she wants to feel loved.

You may want to skip over this part and just get into the "action" part, but this is a very important action you should take.

Later in the book you'll get access to a list of responses from a survey shared with 1,000s of women that will give you a general idea of when women feel loved. This list is NOT to replace your wife's list.

No one can tell you exactly how your wife feels loved, besides your wife. The list you'll have access to is just to help spark ideas.

This book is not to tell you exactly what to do to show your wife you love her on purpose. This book and the Husband On Purpose Alliance is here to help you along your journey of discovering things you can do that can help you show your wife you love her on purpose.

You have to actually discover and do them yourself though.

3

Be Humble, Be Courageous

Marriage is a commitment to seek each other's well-being.
- **Dr. Gary Chapman**

Have you ever wanted to read your wife's mind? If you haven't, she's wanted you to. Getting feedback in your marriage is like reading your wife's mind.

Asking your wife for feedback, possibly, shows a commitment to seeking her well-being.

Implementing what she says and having conversations about what she says, absolutely, shows a commitment to seeking her well-being.

This is basically like "cheating" in marriage. Have you ever felt like you're being tested in your marriage? Well this is a way to be better prepared for those "tests".

The second most important thing that you do in this step is ask your wife for feedback, even though it's the first thing you have to do.

The first most important thing you do is actually be humble

enough and courageous enough to listen to her feedback and implement and integrate the feedback she gives into your everyday life.

You have to be humble enough to accept what she is saying is true, or may be true if you don't agree with it. Then it's going to take courage to DO what she's saying.

There have been things that my wife has told me about myself that I absolutely did not agree with. In the beginning of marriage I would resist, fight back, and be combative.

Then one day I realized that doesn't help at all. It takes me a while sometimes, but eventually I catch on. Eventually.

Even if I don't agree at all with what she is, or was, saying needs to be changed, I need to listen to what she is saying and take it into consideration. I had to read that last sentence twice. Or more.

Is it possible that what she is saying is true in any way, shape, form or fashion? Yes.

Is it possible that it's not true for me and at the same time true for her? Yes.

Is it possible that I'm ever wrong in my marriage? Yes, no matter how bad I try not to be.

One husband I talked to about starting the program told me he already knows what he needs to do better in his marriage. That is irrelevant.

He was using the four worst words in the English language.

"I already know that."

He could've been using more powerful words.

"Am I doing that?"

Which could have led to even more powerful words,

"How can I get better or do that better?"

Don't be like that guy. Humble yourself and ask your wife what you could do better. If you want to feel good when she answers this question, wait until after you've already doing your 30 Day Challenge for a little while.

Here's what worked for me. I was almost done with my first challenge and I sent Jennifer another email saying…

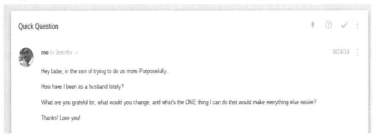

"Hey babe, I'm just trying to do US more Purposefully, how have I been as a husband lately? What are you grateful for, what would you change, and what's the ONE thing I can do that would make everything else easier?"

WINNER WINNER WINNER WINNER WINNER

I call it a winner for a few reasons. She gave me some pretty great praise which made me feel good. She also gave me something to improve on which I was able to use before my 30 day challenge was over.

Eventually your wife may beat you to the punch. Jennifer has come back at me with just about every question I've asked her and sometimes it's hard to answer these questions.

One time it took me a week to answer the feedback question. Later in the book you'll learn how Ben Franklin can help make this a habit so it becomes easier.

This question is not necessarily easy to answer at times. Give your wife some grace in answering this question.

If she needs a little time that's fine. Don't let her off completely though.

What could be more purposeful than being proactive in your marriage? Instead of letting things blow up or get too far, you address the mole-hill before it becomes a mountain.

33

Hopefully by the time you ask this question your wife's love tank will be pretty full and she'll give you some praise and give you a boost of confidence.

This question will also help push you through the 30 Day challenge. Your wife may give you new things you could work on. Or she may tell you how you can be better at the things you have been working on.

The great thing about this question is it goes beyond the 30 Day Challenge. You can ask this question 60 days later, five months later, or four years later. And you should. In a few pages you'll learn a version you can ask on a weekly basis.

Is it possible that six months down the road your wife won't feel loved the same way she does today? Absolutely!

So when you ask that feedback question, you can ALWAYS "cheat' and know what will make your wife feel loved on purpose. The feedback is good for both of you and keeps you being a Husband On Purpose and not just "checking things off of a list".

It's easy to fall back into the mundane comfort zone of a rut. This feedback question will help you avoid that.

We all usually go back to what's comfortable to us. Having continual feedback keeps you honest and keeps you on track.

This question also lets your wife know that you are trying. You are telling her you're trying and telling her she is important to you.

You're telling her you're being intentional about her. You're not saying those words directly to her, but that's exactly what she's hearing.

When you show your wife you're trying to be purposeful, hopefully your wife will appreciate it and try to be more purposeful as well.

The feedback may not always be comfortable. That's good.

It gives us an opportunity to grow.

"A person's success in life can usually be measured by the number of uncomfortable conversations he or she is willing to have." - **Tim Ferriss**

Your success in your marriage can also be measured by the number of uncomfortable conversations you are willing to have.

4

Exactly How to Speak

(Action Steps)

1. Send your wife The Challenge Question so you can Speak Her Dialect.
2. Make a list of the ways that she knows she feels loved and keep it in a handy place. Your phone or the next section in this book is a great place.
3. Come up with actual ways you can DO what is on her list.

You'll need 30 of them for your 30 Day Challenge.

My Wife Knows I Love Her When...

_____

_____

_____

_____

_____

_____

_____

_____

_____

_____

_____

_____

_____

_____

_____

_____

30 Ways I Can Speak Her Dialect

1. _____

2. _____

3. _____

4. _____

5. _____

6. _____

7. _____

8. _____

9. _____

10. _____

11. _____

12. _____

13. _____

14. _____

15. _____

16. _____

17. _____

18. _____

19. _____

20. _____

21. _____

22. _____

23. _____

24. _____

25. _____

26. _____

27. _____

28. _____

29. _____

30. _____

Her Answers and Your Actions will have a huge impact on your marriage. The 30 Day Challenge section is in just a few pages, but there's more you should know before you go there.

There's a "missing ingredient" that helped me stay on track with my 30 Day Challenge.

This next section is all about how this missing ingredient is going to help you do the same.

Six Steps

and

31 Questions to

D.I.S.A.R.M.

B.S. Mediocrity

From Your Marriage

5
The Missing Ingredient

No matter what we're doing in life or what situation we're in, there's something that plays a big role in how we live. So many times we want to go from idea straight to tactic or strategy. Many of us miss an important part in the middle though.

There's something we need to work on along the way or other changes are irrelevant most of the time. This is the factor that will help us along the path no matter what journey we're on.

Here's how it works on the marriage journey. We get married. We know what we want. We want a good marriage. We want a great marriage.

We want a marriage that makes us feel good. We want a marriage that makes our wife feel good. We want to feel love. We want to feel respect. We want to feel secure. We start off pretty good.

At some point things start to go a little downhill. We look for answers. We go to counseling. We listen to radio shows. We listen to podcasts. We read books. We're looking for tactics and strategies that we can implement.

We find the strategies. We implement these strategies. Things go good for a little while. Things are looking like our relationship is on the rise.

We start to feel good. We start to feel loved. We're feeling respected. We're feeling secure.

Then... we hit a snag. We have an argument. We don't feel loved. We don't feel secure. We don't feel respected.

What happened!?

We implemented a strategy. But our mindset never changed.

We started to take different actions, but without the purpose of changing our own mindset.

The actions are important. The tactics and strategies are important. However, without a changed mindset there will never be lasting change.

My goal in the following pages is to help you shift your mindset to a higher level. The purpose of the actions is really to shift your mindset. The purpose of shifting your mindset is to really shift your actions.

If you pay attention to your mindset and your actions you can be on an upward spiral in your marriage. You can continually get better.

D.I.S.A.R.M. B.S. Mediocrity

B.S. = BELOW STANDARDS. You've got to have standards for your marriage. On a scale of 1 - 10, 1 being the worst and 10 being the best, you have to decide what kind of marriage you want. Or whatever scale you want to use.

If you're reading this you likely want a 10 or higher. If a 10 is what you want, that's the standard you set for your marriage. Then you decide you won't settle for anything below standards. You won't settle for B.S.

Anything below standards is mediocrity or worse. No one wants a mediocre or worse marriage or any area of life for that matter. Here are six steps I learned in a business training that I apply to different areas of my life. These six steps helped me publish this book.

The biggest area it's helped me though, is in being a better husband.

This section is all about you. It's all about what you can do for you.

These steps helped me become a better man and helped me stay consistent with being a Husband On Purpose.

They've helped other people and they will help you too, if

you let them.

The foundation of these steps came from a training with a guy named Jon Berghoff. He's not that easy of a guy to get access to, but I'm fortunate that my coach is his best friend.

That is also fortunate for you. Let's dive in!

Decide Dream

I've learned that people will forget what you said, people will forget what you did, but people will never forget how you made them feel. - **Maya Angelou**

The first step is to decide on and dream about the marriage you want to have. You must set some goals for your marriage. Think about what you want your marriage to look like.

Ask yourself…

1. What is the ideal outcome I want from my marriage?
2. How do I want to feel?
3. How do I want my wife to feel?

What do I mean by how do I want me and my wife to feel?

I mean how you want to feel when you think about your wife or when you're around your wife.

I mean how you want your wife to feel when she thinks about you or is around you.

I would see these things and try to really FEEL what it would be like to EXPERIENCE the way I really wanted my marriage to be.

In a Wall Street Journal article, Bosch said 40% of Americans fight about loading the dishwasher. Jennifer and I were in that 40%.

I don't know if we ever really "fought" over loading the dishwasher, but we definitely have had some silly disagreements and unnecessary arguments over simple stuff, including loading the dishes.

<Begin Sarcasm> Obviously the plastics are supposed to go on the top rack and the plates are supposed to face to the right because that's how I learned how to do it. <End Sarcasm>

When I decided there were certain ways and things I wanted Jennifer to feel when she thought about me, I let the trivial dishwasher disagreement go.

I didn't want someone to mention my name and the thing that comes to her mind is "He fusses about how I load the dishes!"

I didn't want someone to mention her name and what comes to my mind is "She puts the plastics on the bottom!"

The truth is that's what happens though. What we focus on expands and how we make someone feel becomes who we are to them.

Deciding on and dreaming about your ideal marriage gives you something to strive for. And a standard to uphold.

This is not to say we're dreaming about a new marriage and are ungrateful for our current marriage.

Decide on and dream about the marriage you want while being grateful for the marriage you have.

Here's an interesting exercise.

Start with the end in mind.

Imagine your wife at your funeral. I know that can sound, well, morbid, but stay with me for a second.

What would you want your wife to say about you at your funeral?

What kind of man do you want her to remember you as?

What kind of man do you want her to tell everyone you were?

How do you want her to say you made her feel?

That's the life you want to live with her NOW.

I ntegrity

Self-Discipline is doing what you need to do, when you need to do it, no matter how you feel. – **Hal Elrod**

Integrity is all about Doing What's Right, Not What's Easy. Ask yourself...

4.   What is the right thing for me to do in my marriage?

5.   What is the easy thing for me to do?

6.   What am I choosing to do?

It's about doing what I need to do when I need to do it even when I don't feel like doing it.

I had to choose the long term success of my marriage over

temporary personal pleasure.

So what's right for my marriage? In general, the right things to do are anything moving me towards being a better husband, loving my wife on purpose, and building a better marriage.

What's right for your marriage?

I needed to do the things on my wife's list, no matter what. I needed to make sure I was being purposeful about it.

I needed to make sure I was doing the Right thing and not the Easy thing.

I constantly reminded myself to choose to Do What's Right Not What's Easy by setting several alarms on my phone throughout the day that had the words, "Do What's Right Not What's Easy", pop up on my screen.

I'd repeat those words to myself 10 times and reflect over the time period since the last alarm and ask myself, did I do the right things or the easy things?

 acrifice

Great achievement is usually born of great sacrifice, and is never the result of selfishness. – **Napoleon Hill**

Ask yourself...

7. What am I willing to give up for the marriage I say I want?

8. Is there a mindset I need to give up?

9. Is there an emotion or a behavior I need to give up?

10. Is there a relationship I need to be willing to let go of?

There were several for me. I had to decide, I love my wife, myself, my marriage, and what my marriage represents more than those other things.

What can you give up to free up time to dedicate to loving your wife?

What can you give up that will free up some of your headspace and allow you to be more creative when it comes to loving your wife?

Decide on something you're going to give up and replace it for the next 30 days with purposefully loving your wife. Test and see if it helps your marriage.

What habit do you have that is not a priority and can be replaced with the higher priority of loving your wife?

Even if it's just five days, if you would normally spend 30 minutes per day on that habit, invest those 30 minutes into your marriage.

Do something with and/or for your wife instead. This was a common answer in the survey sent to over 1,000 women. Generally women feel loved when you do something with and/or for them that you wouldn't normally do.

Have a meaningful conversation with her. Exercise together. Draw a picture together. Cook a meal together. Have passionate sex with each other. Write her a love note. Write a song for her. Collaborate with someone else to create a gift for her. Plan out a date night or a vacation. Get down to the fine details and present it to her.

Just do something with or for your wife during the time you would normally be doing the habit you are sacrificing.

What are you willing to sacrifice to become a better man and build a better marriage?

Align

If you can tune into your purpose and really align with it [...] then life flows much more easily. – **Jack Canfield**

Ask yourself…

11. Do my behaviors, my environment, my mentality, my skills, my learning, my knowledge, all align with the marriage I say I want?

12. Additionally, are my actions aligned with what I say I want in my marriage?

13. Am I hanging around people who are in

alignment with what I say I want?

14. Are the things I'm reading and listening to in alignment with what I want?

For the next 30 days, and hopefully beyond then, everything needs to be in alignment with being a better man and building a better marriage.

Your effectiveness and consistency during your 30 Day Challenge is also affected by your alignment. It will help you to align who you are with what you're doing.

The first rule of sustainability is to align with natural forces, or at least not try to defy them. – **Paul Hawken**

Ask yourself...

15. Am I using my abilities to show my love to my wife?

What are you good at? Writing, creating, talking, singing, fixing things, what?

Leverage who you are already, to really crush this challenge and wow your wife.

Aligning yourself with the right things is important. Perhaps misaligning yourself from the wrong things is more important.

Ask Yourself...

16. What is not in alignment with what I'm saying I want?

17. What am I taking in that is not in alignment with what I say I want?

18. What am I hearing, what am I watching, what am I thinking, what am I believing, what
56

am I saying, what am I doing that is not in alignment with what I say I want?

Let those things go now. Allow yourself to be attached to everything that is in alignment with being a better man and building a better marriage.

Whenever I have a Husband On Purpose Conversation with someone, usually the person I'm speaking with says one of the biggest factors that helps them be a Husband On Purpose is being around other men who are trying to be a Husband On Purpose.

There is an invitation for you later in this book to align yourself with other men just like you in the Husband On Purpose Alliance.

R eflect

By three methods we may learn wisdom: First, by reflection...
- Confucius

EVERYDAY you have to look back and give yourself feedback. Multiple times per day, reflect. That's what you do with your Do What's Right Not What's Easy alarm.

Don't go long without looking back and getting feedback. Evaluate how well you are doing at being a better man and building a better marriage.

Ask Yourself...

19. What's working and not working?

20. What have I learned and what could I do

differently?

21. What am I going to do differently?

Another, perhaps even more important way to reflect is to reflect on the meanings you are giving situations or words.

"Without reflection, we go blindly on our way, creating more unintended consequences, and failing to achieve anything useful." – **Margaret J. Wheatly**

Ask Yourself…

22. What meaning am I giving what I just experienced?

23. Why am I giving it that meaning?

24. Is there a more beneficial meaning I could give to the experience?

25. What do I need to change in terms of how I'm looking at this situation right now?

A friend of mine told me that his job actually encouraged this principle with an acronym. AAPI. Always Assume Positive Intent.

Reflecting on the meaning I'm giving things is helping me in a lot of areas in my life. During my original 30-Day Challenge, I really learned the value of reflection on the meanings I gave things.

One morning I went to fill up the gas tank and have the car cleaned before Jennifer had a busy day of driving around. One of the things on her list that showed her she was loved was "being thoughtful", so I was being thoughtful and showing her I loved her.

I felt really good about myself. It made me happy to make her happy. I just knew she was going to appreciate what I was doing. Then I got a text that changed my whole mood.

The car wash was broken and washing the car was taking longer than it should have. I was surprising Jennifer so all she knew was that I was running a quick errand.

She texts me asking "Where are you? What's taking you so long? Are you getting me coffee?" Obviously you can't hear her tone of voice by reading the words on this page, but imagine she's saying it in an annoying, nagging, negative tone.

Unfortunately, that is what I imagined. Even though just like you, I had no idea what tone of voice she sent that text message in.

Immediately I'm thinking, *"Oh she's being ungrateful, checking up on me, when I'm trying to do something nice for her!"*

Then I paused and said to myself, *"Wait a minute! That's just the meaning I'm giving to what I read."*

I immediately turned it around and said to myself, *"Oh she misses me, she loves me, and she's concerned about me."*

My whole attitude changed. I would have went home defensive with an attitude. She would've asked me what's wrong. I would've lied and said *"Nothing!"*

We likely would have had an argument and started the day horribly! All based on the meaning that I gave what I read. Instead, I went home and we had a very loving morning. I don't know what her meaning, or tone of voice, was behind the text she sent me.

And it didn't matter. Because of the meaning I assigned to it, I responded in a loving way and we had a loving interaction.

Reflecting on the meanings we give to things definitely makes a difference.

You can continue with unintended consequences failing to achieve anything useful, OR, you can be a Husband On Purpose.

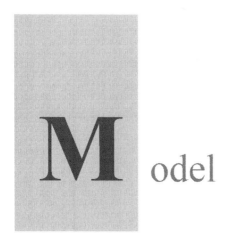

Model

One of the best things you can do for yourself, should you want to improve [...], is figure out models and/or find passive mentors. – **Chris Brogan**

This last step is not for you if you already know everything. This last step is about modeling after men you see that have attributes you like.

Ask Yourself...

26. Who do I want to model the way they treat their wife?

27. How quickly and aggressively can I emulate how they think and what they do?

Find these men and invite them into your life.

I modeled after a few friends I've seen interact with their wives. I chose different attributes from each. One serves his wife very well. One speaks very highly of his wife. One just exudes love for his wife and cherishes her. One has tons of respect for his wife and leads her very well. I tried to model each of these things from them.

I also tried to model me. The Level 10 me.

Think about your future self. The ideal you that you saw in the first step of DISARM.

Ask Yourself…

28. What does the Level 10 me as a husband think, say, and do in this situation?

29. What does the Level 10 me as a husband not do in this situation?

30. What am I doing currently that the Level 10 me doesn't do and what am I currently not doing that the Level 10 me does do?

31. When I'm giving less than Level 10 effort, what am I thinking about and how am I seeing my wife and my life?

7

Obligation or Opportunity

Loving your wife on purpose is an opportunity for you to become a better man. It's an opportunity to help your wife become a better woman. It's an opportunity for both of you to grow. It's an opportunity to improve your kids' lives by setting an example. It's an opportunity to make your community better. It's an opportunity to make the world better.

You have to see this as an opportunity. Here are a few bonus questions to help.

32. Am I looking at my wife and my life as a cause for annoyance or a cause for gratitude? Do I only see an obligation or an opportunity?

33. Do I see loving my wife the way she wants to be loved as an obligation to be annoyed by or an opportunity to be grateful for?

A big part of what I did for 30 days was answer the D.I.S.A.R.M. questions for myself and then meditate on and think about those things pretty frequently throughout the 30 days. Some of them I did once per day and others I did multiple times per day.

The key was scheduling a few minutes each day to doing it. For me, during My Miracle Morning worked best. I took the morning to go through the DISARM acronym and during the day I did the ONE Thing to show her I loved her, every day. That's what my 30 Day Challenge consisted of.

Now is your opportunity to do the same thing.

Your

30 Day

Challenge

8

Your Hero Story

No one can be the hero in your marriage besides you.
— **Husband On Purpose**

This is where you have the opportunity to be the "hero" your wife wants you to be. As Joe Rogan would put it, ***Be the Hero of Your Own Movie.***

Imagine a movie about you and your wife.

The antagonist in the movie is bad communication, pride, fear, undealt with issues, no purposeful love, and everything else that's making you suck as a husband.

The hero is great communication.

The hero is humility.

The hero is courage.

The hero is love.

The hero is You.

Not a prideful, conceited, "I'm the man" look what I did, you.

A humble, serving, courageous, purposeful, loving you.

How does your movie end?

What struggles did you (the hero) face? What challenges do you (the hero) overcome?

What are the easy things you (the hero) could have done, but you made a decision not to do?

What are things that were hard for you to do, and you made a decision to do them anyway?

What did you have to give up?

What did you do on a daily basis to cultivate being the hero you were expected to be?

What meanings did you give situations?

What Level 10 Thoughts and Actions did you take and what lower level Thoughts and Actions did you give up?

Write this story out. This is your hero story. Your wife and everyone else around you will thank you.

No one can be the hero in your marriage besides you.

What is Your Hero Story? Write it out.

9

Your Challenge to Be Committed

There's two ways to learn: passively and aggressively.
— **James Altucher**

You've passively started to learn about being a Husband On Purpose by reading this book. Your 30-Day Challenge is your opportunity to aggressively learn about being a Husband On Purpose.

Right now, it's all information in your head. Having the information is good, but taking the action and completing your 30-Day Challenge is what gives you the opportunity to be a "hero" to your wife.

Over the next 30 days you are challenged to be committed to your wife.

You are challenged to Love Your Wife on Purpose. To love her how she wants to be loved.

Grow. Be humbly courageous.

Look at her dialect list. Pray over it. Meditate on it. Get your creative juices flowing.

Make a list of as many specific things you can from her list. As you're doing Your 30 Day Challenge more ideas may come to you.

Great! Integrate those ideas in your current list.

Your Husband On Purpose - 30 Day Challenge is a commitment.

You are taking on the commitment of loving your wife on purpose every single day for 30 days.

You are taking on the commitment of discovering how your wife needs and wants to be loved.

You are taking on the commitment of feeling how you want to feel in your marriage, and feeling how you want your wife to feel in your marriage.

You are taking on the commitment of doing what's right, not what's easy, to doing that thing that makes you a better man and better husband, to doing things that will improve your marriage.

You are taking on the commitment to giving up things that are hurting your marriage, a commitment to giving up ego, a commitment to giving up pride, maybe relationships, and maybe selfishness.

You are taking on the commitment of aligning your thoughts, actions, and influences with what you say you want.

You are taking on the commitment to reflecting on the meaning you're giving things, and a commitment to giving things beneficial meanings.

You are taking on the commitment to modeling your Level 10 self, modeling different aspects of people you admire, and doing things the Level 10 you would do and stopping things the Level 10 you wouldn't do.

You are taking on a commitment to an obligation with actions to match.

A commitment, by definition, is an obligation that restricts your freedom. When you are committed there are certain actions you can and cannot take.

Your 30-Day Challenge should not be an obligation that annoys you. You have to decide to do this because you want to.

You should see it as an obligation that provides you the opportunity to grow.

It is an obligation that provides you the opportunity to help your wife in a way that is most beneficial to her. It is an opportunity to help create a great home environment.

Your freedom is restricted by choice because you want to grow, you want to be beneficial to your wife, and you want to create a great home environment.

You're choosing to be obligated because of the great opportunity.

You're choosing to be committed.

One question that comes up and you may have the same question is, how do I do this 30 Day challenge without my wife knowing?

You may have a wife who could have the tendency to try and "call you out", or make you feel bad, or do anything to make it harder. I didn't tell Jennifer about what I was doing originally and part of the reason was that is how I felt.

Part of it was I wanted to see if I could make a difference in our relationship just by changing me, my thoughts and my actions. I wanted to see how what I was doing really affected her.

The other part of it was I didn't really trust her to just let me do it. I didn't want her to hold me accountable.

We are at a point in our relationship now where I do trust her enough to let her in on what I'm doing. My increase in trust has nothing to do with who she is or what she does though.

I've matured more and I'm not afraid of her feedback anymore. I'm not afraid of, and I even welcome, her accountability now.

Your situation is your situation.

You have to decide whether or not to tell your wife what you're doing. Maybe you don't tell her everything you're doing with the DISARM steps.

But it may be beneficial to let her know that you want to be a Husband On Purpose and want to make sure she knows she's loved and you're challenging yourself to show her this for the next 30 days.

10

Your First One Percent

It could be hard to find time to go through the DISARM steps and look at your wife's list.

Be the hero of your story and figure out how to make it happen.

Make it a priority. For me the best thing was to include it in My Miracle Morning routine.

Fifteen minutes is approximately 1% of your day. Does your marriage and your wife deserve to at least have 1% of your day dedicated to them?

That leaves you 99% of your day to do whatever you want.

Spend five to fifteen minutes praying, meditating, and thinking about how you want your marriage to be. Spend time thinking about how you want to feel and how you want your wife to feel.

Feel yourself feeling that way.

See you and her enjoying each other, at peace, full of love and respect.

Go through your DISARM questions and go over her list.

You can literally take 60 Seconds with her list and make a huge difference.

For **60 Seconds Daily** look at her list and pray over it.

Ask Yourself...

"Am I Doing This?"

If no, "How Can I Do This?"

If yes, "How Can I Improve This?"

Another good activity during your focused time is to write down one thing you're grateful for about your wife. Don't just write it down though.

Take a moment and really focus on it. Smile. Feel what that thing makes you feel like. Feel it in your whole body.

Next take some time to think about what the Level 10 you would do to make TODAY a great day with and for your wife. See yourself doing that thing with joy and pleasure.

See your wife receiving your actions with joy and pleasure. Feel what that feels like.

These are also things you can do right after you get off work, before you get home. It should be a priority and is a great way to start your day in the morning, but it's also something you can do when you need to "switch gears" and go from work mode to home mode.

60 Second Turn Around

Another great use of 60 seconds is to go through DISARM spending 10 seconds on each step.

It changes your whole outlook, demeanor, and I think even physiology.

You can do it as you're pulling in the driveway from work, you can do it in the middle of a conversation, or whenever you need a quick turnaround.

Ask to be excused for one moment, say *"You know what, can*

you give me about 90 seconds to respond, I just need a moment to think about a few things."

If you want to, close your eyes. Or sit there with your eyes open.

Ask yourself, how do I want my wife to feel and/or how do I want to feel in the long term?

What do I need to do for long term success and fulfilment, what's the right thing to do that's going to move us forward?

What do I need to give up or let go of to get what I'm saying I want?

What beliefs, behaviors, words, actions, etc. align with what I'm saying I want?

What beneficial meaning can I give this situation right now?

What would "so and so" advise me to do right now?

What does the Level 10 me do in this situation?

It works for me. I promise you. Test it for yourself.

11

Your BEST Is Not Required

To get good results and have a good marriage, your best is not required...

You just have to be good.

So it's totally up to you to be proactive and give your best.

You have to decide you're going to give your marriage your all, 100%, no matter what your spouse is doing or does. You have to realize and accept that you are ultimately responsible for your marriage.

Your marriage can't be 50/50. The problem with 50/50 is your 50 is contingent upon her 50. The same goes for 100/100.

You have to have the 100/0 Mindset. Giving your all can't be contingent upon her giving anything. This is not to say let her run all over you, or you just do everything forever and she does nothing.

An important part of having a 100/0 Mindset is knowing you will not always give the same 100%. If you do, that's wonderful, but if you don't, welcome to life on earth.

The goal is to strive to give 100% despite what your wife is giving and despite how you feel.

Don't have an "All or Nothing" mentality. That's only okay if you realize your "All" is not the same all the time.

Don't use "all or nothing" as an excuse. Don't say I can't do this "all" so I'm not going to do anything.

Do all you can do. You have to be okay with your all being different from day to day and okay with your 100% not always looking exactly the same.

This is not to say to use that as an excuse to do less, but to be okay with your 100% being different at different times.

"Did I do my best?"

I used to think "success" took doing "whatever it takes."

Then I heard someone say, "You do your best until your best is not enough. Then you do whatever it takes."

Sometimes success does take "whatever it takes". Sometimes it only takes our best.

For years I've been being taught the second step. Then one day Jeff Goins taught me the importance of stressing the first step first.

Jeff's dad asked him on a regular basis, *"Did you do your best?"* Whether he got fantastic results like all A's or horrid results like all F's, his dad asked *"Did you do your best?"*

That's all that mattered.

Good results, and sometimes even great results, don't always require our best effort.

Most relationships can survive on mediocre effort.

The best results and the best marriage require your best effort.

Ask yourself constantly, "Did I do my best?"

You'll do better at staying on track of giving 100% to your marriage.

Husband on Purpose is about becoming a better you and

purposefully loving your wife.

It's about becoming a better you WHILE purposefully loving your wife and becoming a better you THROUGH purposefully loving your wife.

It's about the commitment and the obligation of being a husband. You have to decide you're going to be the change maker in your marriage. You have to take full responsibility for your marriage.

If you're in a drastic situation, like an abusive marriage, get professional help from the right people.

If your marriage is just "okay" or even good, but could be better, do what you learn in Husband On Purpose.

This is about having a Slight Edge marriage and making your marriage better consistently. It's about being the hero your wife wants you to be through small, consistent, purposeful actions.

Being a hero doesn't mean some dramatic feat. Being a hero is doing what the other person thought couldn't be done. You can "wow your wife" through consistency.

Give it 100%. Give it your Best.

The

Ben Franklin

Method

To Being a

Husband

On Purpose

12

One Simple Change

What do you do after you complete your first Husband On Purpose – 30 Day Challenge?

You may decide to do it again. Here's another option.

The Ben Franklin method shows you how to take 45 minutes per week and build a strong foundation for a better bond and clearer communication with your wife.

Ben used this method himself to acquire what he called *"the essential principles of successful living."*

I learned about this method in Frank Bettger's *How I Raised Myself from Failure to Success in Selling*. Frank says the chapter he wrote about this method was the most important chapter in his entire book.

Benjamin Franklin wrote more about this method than any other subject in his autobiography. He felt he owed all of his success and happiness to this.

I used it in my own life when I was trying to strengthen my relationship with God. This method gave me a simple and effective plan to build a strong foundation in my own life and it has helped many others.

It's a proven method. Test it in your marriage.

What's the Ben Franklin Method?

"Franklin chose 13 subjects which he felt were necessary or desirable for him to acquire and try to master, and he gave a week's strict attention to each subject successively."

I call it "One Simple Change"

That's what it's about.

Giving a week's strict attention to One Simple Change.

That's it.

Focus on ONE simple change. Do it every day for a week.

The idea to use this in marriage came to me when Jennifer sent me a text asking, "What is the ONE thing I can do that can make things easy for you?"

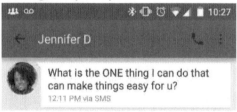

She learned that from somewhere. ☺

When she asked this, I began to think about "What could she do right now?"

The thing I thought of was super simple. Just a simple change.

I knew that the one thing she could do next week may be different. So why not just proactively use the Ben Franklin method like I had before?

This is a way to consistently be proactive and purposeful in your marriage.

How?

Get clearly focused on what the change is.

Keep it simple. Be specific.

Simple is relative. Simple for you may be difficult for me. Simple may be something you can do with very little extra effort or no extra effort at all.

Specific is important. We found this out with my very first suggestion.

I suggested going to bed on time was a simple change that could make things easier for me.

The next day we had an argument because I was up later than what Jennifer thought I meant by going to bed on time.

Be clear about your One Simple Change.

Being clear will help you actually do it and help you communicate better.

Instead of "go to bed on time", I should of said "go to bed at <enter specific time>."

To decide on your One Simple Change, have a conversation with your wife and ask each other the following question.

What's One Simple Change we can make this week to make things easier, interesting, or exciting?

You can either choose something you're going to do together or something each of you will do for each other.

Once you decide on your One Simple Change, make a clear commitment to doing it.

Commit to what you're doing and why you're doing it. Follow the template below.

"We are committed to <ENTER YOUR ONE SIMPLE CHANGE> every day this week so that we can <ENTER A DIRECT PRACTICAL REASON> because <ENTER A DEEP-ROOTED REASON>."

Here's an example…

We are committed to going to bed at 10pm every day this week except Friday so that we can wake up on time with energy and in good moods because it helps us start our day much better and when we start our days better, our days are better overall.

Discuss your One Simple Change before you start your week for 15 minutes to really narrow it down to one simple change.

If Sunday is the beginning of your week, discuss it on Saturday.

This is a time for you to choose One Simple Change that will make things easier, more interesting, or more exciting.

This is also the time to figure out WHY you're making this One Simple Change.

This is also the time to narrow down your One Simple Change.

Maybe your One Simple Change is being on time every day this week. Focus that down more. Maybe One Simple Change could be use Google Maps to calculate how long it will take to get everywhere we're going this week and leave 10 minutes before it says we need to leave.

Your commitment looks like this,

We are committed to leaving 10 minutes earlier than Google Maps says we need to leave to get everywhere we're going this week so that we can be early because that shows respect for our own time and whoever we're meeting and cuts down on any stress and arguments that running late causes us.

That's what you do for 15 minutes on whatever day is the day before you start your week.

The other 6 days of the week, spend 5 minutes with your spouse discussing how your One Simple Change is going.

How has doing it made things easier, more interesting, or more exciting?

What could we change in how we do it to make it better, if anything?

How is this moving us closer to our Why of doing it?

These can be quick answers. This part is only supposed to take 5 minutes.

Here are a few reminders to stay on track.

Old School. Tear a piece of cardboard from a box somewhere. Make it small enough to fit in your pocket, but big enough that you notice it in your pocket.

On one side write down your commitment.

On the other side write the questions, Am I doing this? How can I do this better?

New School. Set a few alarms, at least three, on your phone to alert you throughout the day. Have your commitment pop up on your screen. Include the questions "Am I doing this? How can I do this better?"

You can also set up some type of accountability system with another couple or a friend that will check in on a daily basis to see how you're doing.

You may be able to find someone in the Husband On Purpose Alliance.

15 minutes one day per week. 5 minutes the other 6 days per week = 45 minutes per week as a foundation to your One Simple Change.

Some weeks you may have to spend more time actually doing your One Simple Change and some weeks your One Simple Change will actually take up no extra time.

52 Example One Simple Changes

1. Go to bed at a specific time
2. Wake up at a specific time
3. Kiss every time we leave or enter each other's presence
4. Pray together at a specific time each day
5. Have a specific length conversation about a specific topic at a specific time each day
6. Go for a walk at a specific time each morning
7. Leave 15 minutes before we have to get everywhere we're going this week
8. Eat a specific meal together at a specific time
9. Have sex every day this week
10. Watch a movie together every day this week
11. Watch a TV show together
12. Write a handwritten note to each other and give it to each other every night at a specific time
13. Write handwritten notes to other people
14. Workout together
15. Go on a date
16. Meditate together
17. Talk about our dreams
18. Write a story
19. Create a product
20. Buy something for someone else
21. Give something away
22. Buy something for each other
23. Read something
24. Have a conversation with friends
25. Have a conversation with strangers
26. Eat something new
27. Cook something together
28. Cook something new

29. Go to a new store
30. Take a different route
31. Drive to work together
32. Drive one car
33. Walk to work
34. Take public transit
35. Visit a new neighborhood
36. Go look at model homes
37. Have appetizers
38. Have dessert
39. Eat only veggies
40. Volunteer somewhere
41. No TV
42. Pick out each other's clothes
43. Iron each other's clothes
44. Brush each other's teeth
45. Shower together
46. Stay at a hotel/resort
47. Camp out in the living room
48. No social media
49. Meet someone new everyday
50. Play board games (Discovery)
51. Shoot a video
52. Learn something new

These are just 52 random ideas. They are included with the hopes that they spark your imagination. Some of them are very general. Make them specific. Modify them to fit your marriage.

Using One Simple Change is a way to continue being a Husband On Purpose one week at a time. It's good to complete a Husband On Purpose - 30 Day Challenge periodically, maybe 4 times per year, every 90 days. In the between times you can continue to strengthen your marriage with One Simple Change.

You're Invited

I appreciate you taking the time to read this book. Now my hope is that you will implement what you've read.

The words on these pages are just information until you apply them to your life, at which point your experience of applying them becomes knowledge. Knowledge is power. Your own knowledge.

Someone else's knowledge of something is just information to you, until you experience it for yourself. Information is good, but useless until it becomes knowledge.

If you haven't downloaded your Free Husband On Purpose Bonuses do so now. You'll get 12 Months of The Husband On Purpose Journal pages, The Husband On Purpose Worksheets to fill out to help you stay on track, weekly emails sharing interesting stories from other husbands being purposeful about their marriages, and a $100 gift (real world value) reserved only for The Husband On Purpose Community Participants. Download the resources. Join the community. Get the goods. Become a Better Man. Build a Better Marriage

The ACTION you're taking along with developing the right MINDSET is a good start to the recipe of being a Husband On Purpose. The last ingredient is ACCOUNTABILITY.

When you observe and study noteworthy accomplishments that people achieve you'll discover that there is almost always some form of accountability in place.

You can form your own system of accountability or you can join ours in The Husband On Purpose Alliance. The Alliance is for you if you want to be held accountable to being a Husband On Purpose, consistently doing 30 Day Challenges when you need to, and using One Simple Change per week to become a better man and build a better marriage.

We are a growing community of husbands helping each other become better men and build better marriages.

There are additional perks and resources available to Alliance Members that you can find out about after you download your Free Book Resources at

http://HusbandOnPurpose.com/free-book-bonuses

Additional Resources

To download or access the following resources visit **http://HusbandOnPurpose.com/free-book-bonuses**

Husband On Purpose Conversations: This has become one of my most favorite parts about Husband On Purpose besides bettering myself and my marriage. I've been able to connect with some great men who have decided to be purposeful about their own marriages. I'd like to introduce you to a few of them.

How Women Feel Loved: A survey was sent to over 1,000 wives and this resource has answers to The Challenge Question. These are not to be used in place of what your wife said, but as a supplement to spark ideas in your mind. Happy Reading!

The Husband On Purpose 30-Day Challenge and One Simple Change Journal: Easily track your progress on a daily basis. One of the simplest, yet best accountability tools you will have is keeping a daily journal.

List of Marriage Websites, Books, & More: including resources like MarriageWorks.us, Loving Your Wife as Christ Loves The Church, and many more

All of these resources and any I add in the future are available when you visit

http://HusbandOnPurpose.com/free-book-bonuses

Would You Like to Help?

If this book was helpful to you please don't hesitate to leave a review on Amazon so others can know what you thought about Husband On Purpose. Reviews are extremely helpful. Just visit

www.HusbandOnPurpose.com/review

The best thing you can do is tell a friend about *Husband On Purpose*. Maybe that friend will become your accountability partner. The mission of Husband On Purpose is heavily dependent upon Word of Mouth, so if you want to help eliminate (or at least minimize) "Idiot Husband" moments across the globe, tell a friend about this book. For easy ways to share the book visit

www.HusbandOnPurpose.com/team

ACKNOWLEDGEMENTS

To God who created me, thank You. You created me On Purpose, so I intend to Live Everyday On Purpose.

To my biggest supporter, Jennifer, The Love of My Life. This wouldn't have been possible without you. Literally. You are the reason this book came out first. Thank you for forgiving me so many times and allowing me to become better. Clouds are ALWAYS temporary. The sun is ALWAYS shining. I'm excited about our future!

To my parents, without you all I wouldn't be here. Thanks for doing what you did and doing what you do. Love you!

To my siblings, you helped me become who I am. The good and the bad. I like all of me, so thank you :-)

And my extended family. Yes you :-) Much of who I am is a result of where I'm from. You are where I am from. I wouldn't be me, without you.

Artice Barlow and Sonya Cheltenham, thank you for schooling me before I got married on what it means to be married. You told me the truth and for that I am grateful.

Kevin Bullard you and Cetelia have been a blessing to Jennifer and I since the beginning of our marriage. Thank you for encouraging me along this journey and continually pointing me in the right direction.

Donnie Bryant, I'm not sure this would have happened without your encouragement along the way as well. Thank you for trusting and believing in the message enough to invest your resources in this mission. Dina, thank you for allowing him to.

Michael J. Maher, Gary Keller, Jay Papasan, Dean Jackson, Josh Shipp, Hal Elrod, and Jon Berghoff, thank you for either creating or introducing me to tools, concepts, and strategies that I was able to adapt and put to fantastic use in my marriage. Your influence lives on.

Steve Scott, Derek Doepker, Chandler Bolt, Jeff Goins, Mike Koenigs, Akash Karia, Pat Flynn and Tom Morkes thank you for all your book publishing knowledge that you graciously shared with me. I always believed that the book that no one reads is as good as the book that's never written. You all helped make sure that didn't happen with this book.

To my friends I didn't call by name, you are appreciated and loved.

"What is your most valued possession?"
I was asked that question once, and immediately what came to my mind, is my relationships.

The person asking the question was likely looking for a different answer, but I tend to look at things differently.

Family is extremely high on my "hierarchy of focus". My wife and my three sons are the closest things to my heart, right after God. My extended family follows close behind.

I currently live in the beautiful city of Las Vegas, NV. I began growing up in South Carolina, tried to finish in Georgia and Florida, and maybe Las Vegas will be the place it finally happens :-)

I really love people. I find us extremely interesting and I am fascinated by the way our minds work and why we do what we do.

My other fascination is with creating things that encourage, uplift, and educate people. I get a lot of satisfaction from creating.

I'm on a mission to help you **Live Everyday On Purpose.**

The best way I can do that is through the ignition and the fuel to Living Purposefully, **Humble Courage.** From you and me.

I look forward to progressing along this journey of life with you.

Purposefully,

A. Conrad Deas II

Creator, Encourager, Author of *Husband On Purpose*

Book Conrad To Speak!

Get Conrad to speak at your workshop, event, or conference and you're guaranteed to have your attendees thank you, tell you how awesome your conference was, and want to come back next year.

He is available for men's, leadership, and marriage conferences, workshops, trainings, or other events.

To book Conrad, email **GetConrad@HumbleCourage.com**

The

Husband On Purpose

30 Day Challenge

Sample Journal

Husband On Purpose 30-Day Challenge Journal Week 1

Date _0_ / _15_ /20_22_ - __/__/20__

D_____

_____

I_____

_____

S_____

_____

A_____

_____

R_____

_____

M_____

_____

_____

_____

Day 1 Morning

I am grateful for my wife because…

wanted to speak to we and work some things.

That makes me feel....

Happyy and hope ful and that there's hope.

Today the Level 10 me will…

Listen, let her get her frustrations unt. Write and follow up on her requests. She wants space, so I'll give that to her. I will order trees for our home, fix a leaking toilet

Day 1 Evening

How Did I Love My Wife On Purpose Today?

Sarcasm received.. be humble
give space.

What could I have given a more beneficial meaning today?

Day 2 Morning

I am grateful for my wife because…

She talked and cooked for me

That makes me feel….

happy and loved like a partner.

Today the Level 10 me will…

- Be patient
- Prep old metal frame for turn in
- Prep finances — home
- Yard work, water plants
- cook lasagna
- give space.

Day 2 Evening

How Did I Love My Wife On Purpose Today?

_____

_____

_____

_____

_____

_____

What could I have given a more beneficial meaning today?

_____

_____

_____

_____

_____

_____

Day 3 Morning

I am grateful for my wife because…

_____

That makes me feel….

_____

_____

_____

_____

_____

Today the Level 10 me will…

_____

_____

_____

_____

_____

_____

Day 3 Evening

How Did I Love My Wife On Purpose Today?

_____

_____

_____

_____

_____

_____

What could I have given a more beneficial meaning today?

_____

_____

_____

_____

_____

_____

Day 4 Morning

I am grateful for my wife because...

_____

That makes me feel....

_____

_____

_____

_____

Today the Level 10 me will...

_____

_____

_____

_____

_____

_____

Day 4 Evening

How Did I Love My Wife On Purpose Today?

_____

_____

_____

_____

_____

_____

What could I have given a more beneficial meaning today?

_____

_____

_____

_____

_____

_____

Day 5 Morning

I am grateful for my wife because...

_____

That makes me feel....

_____

_____

_____

_____

_____

Today the Level 10 me will...

_____

_____

_____

_____

_____

_____

Day 5 Evening

How Did I Love My Wife On Purpose Today?

_____

_____

_____

_____

_____

_____

What could I have given a more beneficial meaning today?

_____

_____

_____

_____

_____

_____

Day 6 Morning

I am grateful for my wife because...

_____

That makes me feel....

_____

_____

_____

_____

_____

Today the Level 10 me will...

_____

_____

_____

_____

_____

_____

_____

Day 6 Evening

How Did I Love My Wife On Purpose Today?

_____

_____

_____

_____

_____

_____

What could I have given a more beneficial meaning today?

_____

_____

_____

_____

_____

_____

Day 7 Morning

I am grateful for my wife because…

_____

That makes me feel….

_____

_____

_____

_____

_____

Today the Level 10 me will…

_____

_____

_____

_____

_____

_____

Day 7 Evening

How Did I Love My Wife On Purpose Today?

_____

_____

_____

_____

_____

_____

What could I have given a more beneficial meaning today?

_____

_____

_____

_____

_____

_____

Husband On Purpose 30-Day Challenge Journal Week 2

Date___/___/20__ - __/__/20__

D_____

_____

I_____

_____

S_____

_____

A_____

_____

R_____

_____

M_____

_____

_____

_____

Day 8 Morning

I am grateful for my wife because…

_____

That makes me feel....

_____

_____

_____

_____

_____

Today the Level 10 me will…

_____

_____

_____

_____

_____

_____

Day 8 Evening

How Did I Love My Wife On Purpose Today?

_____

_____

_____

_____

_____

_____

What could I have given a more beneficial meaning today?

_____

_____

_____

_____

_____

_____

Day 9 Morning

I am grateful for my wife because…

_____

That makes me feel....

_____

_____

_____

_____

_____

Today the Level 10 me will…

_____

_____

_____

_____

_____

_____

_____

Day 9 Evening

How Did I Love My Wife On Purpose Today?

_____

_____

_____

_____

_____

What could I have given a more beneficial meaning today?

_____

_____

_____

_____

_____

_____

Day 10 Morning

I am grateful for my wife because…

_____

That makes me feel....

_____

_____

_____

_____

_____

Today the Level 10 me will…

_____

_____

_____

_____

_____

_____

_____

Day 10 Evening

How Did I Love My Wife On Purpose Today?

_____

_____

_____

_____

_____

_____

What could I have given a more beneficial meaning today?

_____

_____

_____

_____

_____

Day 11 Morning

I am grateful for my wife because...

_____

That makes me feel....

_____

_____

_____

_____

_____

Today the Level 10 me will...

_____

_____

_____

_____

_____

_____

Day 11 Evening

How Did I Love My Wife On Purpose Today?

_____

_____

_____

_____

_____

_____

What could I have given a more beneficial meaning today?

_____

_____

_____

_____

_____

_____

Day 12 Morning

I am grateful for my wife because...

_____

That makes me feel....

_____

_____

_____

_____

_____

Today the Level 10 me will...

_____

_____

_____

_____

_____

_____

Day 12 Evening

How Did I Love My Wife On Purpose Today?

_____

_____

_____

_____

_____

_____

What could I have given a more beneficial meaning today?

_____

_____

_____

_____

_____

_____

Day 13 Morning

I am grateful for my wife because...

_____

That makes me feel....

_____

_____

_____

_____

Today the Level 10 me will...

_____

_____

_____

_____

_____

_____

Day 13 Evening

How Did I Love My Wife On Purpose Today?

_____

_____

_____

_____

_____

_____

What could I have given a more beneficial meaning today?

_____

_____

_____

_____

_____

_____

Day 14 Morning

I am grateful for my wife because…

_____

That makes me feel….

_____

_____

_____

_____

Today the Level 10 me will…

_____

_____

_____

_____

_____

_____

Day 14 Evening

How Did I Love My Wife On Purpose Today?

_____

_____

_____

_____

_____

_____

What could I have given a more beneficial meaning today?

_____

_____

_____

_____

_____

_____

Husband On Purpose 30-Day Challenge Journal Week 3

Date___/___/20__ - __/__/20__

D_____

_____

I_____

_____

S_____

_____

A_____

_____

R_____

_____

M_____

_____

_____

_____

Day 15 Morning

I am grateful for my wife because...

_____

That makes me feel....

_____

_____

_____

_____

_____

Today the Level 10 me will...

_____

_____

_____

_____

_____

_____

Day 15 Evening

How Did I Love My Wife On Purpose Today?

_____

_____

_____

_____

_____

What could I have given a more beneficial meaning today?

_____

_____

_____

_____

_____

Day 16 Morning

I am grateful for my wife because...

_____

That makes me feel....

_____

_____

_____

_____

Today the Level 10 me will...

_____

_____

_____

_____

_____

_____

Day 16 Evening

How Did I Love My Wife On Purpose Today?

_____

_____

_____

_____

_____

_____

What could I have given a more beneficial meaning today?

_____

_____

_____

_____

_____

_____

Day 17 Morning

I am grateful for my wife because...

_____

That makes me feel....

_____

_____

_____

_____

_____

Today the Level 10 me will...

_____

_____

_____

_____

_____

_____

Day 17 Evening

How Did I Love My Wife On Purpose Today?

_____

_____

_____

_____

_____

_____

What could I have given a more beneficial meaning today?

_____

_____

_____

_____

_____

_____

Day 18 Morning

I am grateful for my wife because…

_____

That makes me feel....

_____

_____

_____

_____

_____

Today the Level 10 me will…

_____

_____

_____

_____

_____

_____

Day 18 Evening

How Did I Love My Wife On Purpose Today?

_____

_____

_____

_____

_____

_____

What could I have given a more beneficial meaning today?

_____

_____

_____

_____

_____

142

Day 19 Morning

I am grateful for my wife because…

_____

That makes me feel....

_____

_____

_____

_____

_____

Today the Level 10 me will…

_____

_____

_____

_____

_____

_____

Day 19 Evening

How Did I Love My Wife On Purpose Today?

_____

_____

_____

_____

_____

_____

What could I have given a more beneficial meaning today?

_____

_____

_____

_____

_____

_____

Day 20 Morning

I am grateful for my wife because…

_____

That makes me feel....

_____

_____

_____

_____

_____

Today the Level 10 me will…

_____

_____

_____

_____

_____

_____

Day 20 Evening

How Did I Love My Wife On Purpose Today?

_____

_____

_____

_____

_____

_____

What could I have given a more beneficial meaning today?

_____

_____

_____

_____

_____

_____

Day 21 Morning

I am grateful for my wife because...

That makes me feel....

Today the Level 10 me will...

Day 21 Evening

How Did I Love My Wife On Purpose Today?

_____

_____

_____

_____

_____

_____

What could I have given a more beneficial meaning today?

_____

_____

_____

_____

_____

_____

Husband On Purpose 30-Day Challenge Journal Week 4

Date___/___/20__ - __/__/20__

D_____

_____

I_____

_____

S_____

_____

A_____

_____

R_____

_____

M_____

_____

_____

_____

Day 22 Morning

I am grateful for my wife because...

_____

That makes me feel....

_____

_____

_____

_____

_____

Today the Level 10 me will...

_____

_____

_____

_____

_____

_____

Day 22 Evening

How Did I Love My Wife On Purpose Today?

_____

_____

_____

_____

_____

_____

What could I have given a more beneficial meaning today?

_____

_____

_____

_____

_____

Husband On Purpose

Day 23 Morning

I am grateful for my wife because…

_____

That makes me feel….

_____

_____

_____

_____

_____

Today the Level 10 me will…

_____

_____

_____

_____

_____

_____

152

Day 23 Evening

How Did I Love My Wife On Purpose Today?

_____

_____

_____

_____

_____

_____

What could I have given a more beneficial meaning today?

_____

_____

_____

_____

_____

_____

Day 24 Morning

I am grateful for my wife because…

_____

That makes me feel….

_____

_____

_____

_____

_____

Today the Level 10 me will…

_____

_____

_____

_____

_____

_____

_____

Day 24 Evening

How Did I Love My Wife On Purpose Today?

_____

_____

_____

_____

_____

_____

What could I have given a more beneficial meaning today?

_____

_____

_____

_____

_____

Day 25 Morning

I am grateful for my wife because...

_____

That makes me feel....

_____

_____

_____

_____

_____

Today the Level 10 me will...

_____

_____

_____

_____

_____

_____

_____

Day 25 Evening

How Did I Love My Wife On Purpose Today?

_____

_____

_____

_____

_____

_____

What could I have given a more beneficial meaning today?

_____

_____

_____

_____

_____

Day 26 Morning

I am grateful for my wife because…

_____

That makes me feel….

_____

_____

_____

_____

_____

Today the Level 10 me will…

_____

_____

_____

_____

_____

_____

_____

Day 26 Evening

How Did I Love My Wife On Purpose Today?

_____

_____

_____

_____

_____

_____

What could I have given a more beneficial meaning today?

_____

_____

_____

_____

_____

_____

Day 27 Morning

I am grateful for my wife because…

_____

That makes me feel....

_____

_____

_____

_____

Today the Level 10 me will…

_____

_____

_____

_____

_____

_____

Day 27 Evening

How Did I Love My Wife On Purpose Today?

_____

_____

_____

_____

_____

_____

What could I have given a more beneficial meaning today?

_____

_____

_____

_____

_____

_____

Day 28 Morning

I am grateful for my wife because...

_____

That makes me feel....

_____

_____

_____

_____

_____

Today the Level 10 me will...

_____

_____

_____

_____

_____

_____

Day 28 Evening

How Did I Love My Wife On Purpose Today?

_____

_____

_____

_____

_____

_____

What could I have given a more beneficial meaning today?

_____

_____

_____

_____

_____

_____

Day 29 Morning

I am grateful for my wife because…

_____

That makes me feel….

_____

_____

_____

_____

_____

Today the Level 10 me will…

_____

_____

_____

_____

_____

_____

_____

Day 29 Evening

How Did I Love My Wife On Purpose Today?

_____

_____

_____

_____

_____

What could I have given a more beneficial meaning today?

_____

_____

_____

_____

_____

Day 30 Morning

I am grateful for my wife because...

_____

That makes me feel....

_____

_____

_____

_____

_____

Today the Level 10 me will...

_____

_____

_____

_____

_____

_____

Day 30 Evening

How Did I Love My Wife On Purpose Today?

_____

_____

_____

_____

_____

_____

What could I have given a more beneficial meaning today?

_____

_____

_____

_____

_____

_____

One Simple Change 4 Week Journal

This week we are committed to

> GOING TO BED BY 10pm EVERYDAY EXCEPT
> FRIDAY AND 11pm ON FRIDAY

so that we can

> WAKE UP ON TIME WITH ENERGY AND IN
> GOOD MOODS

because

> IT HELPS US START OUR DAY MUCH
> BETTER AND WHEN WE START OUR DAYS
> BETTER, OUR DAYS ARE BETTER OVERALL

_____

_____

_____

Monday	Tuesday	Wednesday	Thursday	Friday	Saturday	Sunday
X	X	X	X		X	X

Notes From This Week

We had a really good week. I learned that I just operate better when I get 8 hours of sleep. Having our meals pre-planned really helped. We missed Friday because we had friends in town. Maybe we could prepare better next time, but we had a good time with our friends so it was worth it.

Ideas for Next Week

It would really help us to have our clothes ready for the whole week ahead of time including having them ironed.

One Simple Change Four Week Journal Week 1

This week we are committed to

```
┌─────────────────────────────────────────────┐
│                                               │
│                                               │
│                                               │
│                                               │
└─────────────────────────────────────────────┘
```

so that we can

```
┌─────────────────────────────────────────────┐
│                                               │
│                                               │
│                                               │
│                                               │
└─────────────────────────────────────────────┘
```

because

```
┌─────────────────────────────────────────────┐
│                                               │
│                                               │
│                                               │
│                                               │
└─────────────────────────────────────────────┘
```

_____

_____

_____

Monday	Tuesday	Wednesday	Thursday	Friday	Saturday	Sunday

Notes From This Week

_____

_____

_____

_____

_____

_____

Ideas for Next Week

_____

_____

_____

_____

One Simple Change Four Week Journal Week 2

This week we are committed to

so that we can

because

Monday	Tuesday	Wednesday	Thursday	Friday	Saturday	Sunday

Notes From This Week

_____

_____

_____

_____

_____

_____

Ideas for Next Week

_____

_____

_____

_____

One Simple Change Four Week Journal Week 3

This week we are committed to

so that we can

because

Monday	Tuesday	Wednesday	Thursday	Friday	Saturday	Sunday

Notes From This Week

_____

_____

_____

_____

_____

_____

Ideas for Next Week

_____

_____

_____

_____

One Simple Change Four Week Journal Week 4

This week we are committed to

so that we can

because

Monday	Tuesday	Wednesday	Thursday	Friday	Saturday	Sunday

Notes From This Week

_____

_____

_____

_____

_____

_____

Ideas for Next Week

_____

_____

_____

_____

Made in the USA
Middletown, DE
10 October 2022

12415227R00106